reliving

Alexi Pariag

BookLeaf
Publishing

India | USA | UK

Presentation by *BookLeaf Publishing*

Web: www.bookleafpub.com

E-mail: info@bookleafpub.com

ISBN: 9789357446679

First edition 2022

DEDICATION

i dedicate this book to my dear friend who told
me to become a poemist. i made it :)

PREFACE

there is no real story here, no satisfying ending.
my life is only just beginning, and i can only
write about what i know. what i know is, i've had
depression since i was 14. and let me tell you,
people with depression LOVE to write poems.
so here i am.

Q&A

have you ever thought about it?
do you hear from it as well?
the question no one wants to answer?
what they're too afraid to even ask?
~~do you mean the thought that comes with~~
~~glassy eyes in the middle of the night~~
~~headaches from staying in bed all day~~
~~eyes too tired to cry or close~~
~~lips incapable of spitting out words~~
————i don't know what you mean.
you don't?
i'm sure you will.
anyway, did you consider it?
when it came knocking, did you answer?
and if you let it in, did it stay?
did you push it away, ~~ashamed~~?
or did you set it aside, ~~to think about another time~~?
~~maybe you held it close?~~
~~maybe you invited it?~~
i don't know.

i don't remember.
okay, you don't remember.

~~i'm sure you will.~~
so, has it returned since?
does it leave you alone for a while?
does it creep up on you when you least expect?
does it give you notice before coming around?
does it run through your mind when you let
yourself feel truthfully?

> ~~yes it's always here it's~~
> ~~white noise blocking voices~~
> ~~thoughts playing on a loop~~
> ~~sleep never equating to rest~~
> ~~body numb from inactivity~~
> ~~heart beaten from the dread~~
> ~~lungs emptied of oxygen~~
> i'm not sure.

you're not sure?
you'll have to be sure.
did you ever listen to it?
did you let its noise drown you out?
does it consume you now?
do you like having it here?
do you miss it sometimes?
do you need it?

> ~~it's all i have anymore i know nothing~~
> ~~besides~~
> ~~a familiar face in a crowd~~
> ~~a comfortable habit to fall into~~
> ~~an old friend i depend on~~
> ~~a crutch for my useless legs~~

~~a medication for my aches and pains~~
no.
what do you do when it visits, now?
do you notice when it's gone?
do you care when it's there?
do you even hate it anymore?
do you know the difference between it and you?
do you want this to be who you are?
do you know who you are without it?

don't talk about it when they ask.
you really think they want to know?
when they don't respond, how will you feel?
you're nothing without me.
i'm all that's left.

starve yourself or eat too much.
sleep forever or not at all.
talk to everyone or be alone.
i'm the only thing that will settle it.
i'm all that's left.

the mistakes you've made.
the damage you've done.
no one will help you fix it.
i can bury the messes you created.
i'm all that's left.

are you still here?

~~barely~~
yes.
do you know now?
~~i always did~~
no.
did you do it?
~~i wanted to~~
no.
did you ever try it?
~~of course i tried yes~~
does it matter?
do you think it matters?
~~yes i want you to know it's all that matters~~
not really.
so, is this it?
is this all?
there's nothing else?
~~not for me~~
nothing.
okay.
guess that's all.

handwashing protocol

my hands are bloodied and hurt
we fight too much
and there's not enough soap in the world to make
my hands feel clean
but let's try anyway.
turn on the tap...
"i need you"

...

rinse off the grime...
"i want to be with you"

...

lather with soap...
"i don't know what's best for us"

...

don't stop lathering...
"liking you makes me feel shitty"

...

has happy birthday always been this long?
"i'm trying not to think of you"

...

rinse everything.
how did we do?

my hands still feel dirty
but the blood is gone
and my knuckles are bruised.
tomorrow we will wash our hands again
lather rinse repeat
until we get it right.

barely human.

i don't think i was meant to be.
we're meant to laugh and love and share
experiences and breathe in and out and watch
sunsets and eat junk food and do things.
but my body is decaying, stripped of life and
blood and unable to hold anything good.
my bones are woven with dead vines and wilted
leaves, i am rotting and decomposing all the
time.
i am too empty to contain anything that a human
should have.
where the heart goes, the mind follows, and my
heart stopped beating long ago.
i await the day my skeleton disappears, when i
become nothing and no one remembers me.

feeling.

it's so hard to intentionally remind myself how
intense the human experience can be.
only by accident will i ever be able to
acknowledge that my feelings and emotions are
as vivid and coloured as i allow them to be.
i feel it when i stand on my kitchen tiles letting
the warmth of the sun pouring through the big
windows wash over me.
i feel it when i press the heels of my hands
against my eyelids and see television static and
what it feels like when my leg falls asleep.
i feel it when my heart begins to beat at the
speed of a helicopter propeller and my stomach
turns over the thought of someone new.
sometimes, i close my eyes in the middle of the
woods, with the wind rushing and the birds
chirping, and i feel like i could live a whole
different life. i feel relieved. i feel it then, too.
i feel it when the leaves crunch, and the grass
pulls out of the ground in tufts, and the sky
drizzles before the torrential downpour, and the
trees let the leaves go even though it was their
only protection against the winds. the bark
softens and the trunk holds even through the
heavy snowfalls and the biting cold, and the

leaves come back in the spring, thankful for the
temporary home the trees provide.
i feel my heart fill up when she remembers how
much i love honey, and he follows up on our
conversations, and she hugs me the next time
she sees me, and he helps me even when i'm
angry. i feel the recognition of love, the displays
of implicit affection, the acknowledgement that
they care. and i feel it heavily.
i have always worn my heart on my sleeve, and i
have always felt deeply. and sometimes that
means that stepping in a puddle and soaking my
shoes is going to be the last straw. but
sometimes it means that petting a dog is going to
jolt me out of my sadness.
the intensity of our emotions is as much as we
allow it. we all limit it, to whatever degree we
feel is safe. the showing of passion is so
desperately feared, mostly because of the
openness necessary for it. vulnerability creates
so much opportunity for pain. and i spend a lot
of time trying to block any chinks in my armor,
and hold back the flood of emotions. but
sometimes, i want to let it go. i want to feel so
much that the sun warms my bones and the rain
hydrates my skin, i want to lay my palm on a
tree's trunk and feel its heartbeat. i want to feel
more than ever before. and i wish that didn't feel
so wrong.

shipwrecked.

shipwrecked seems too violent a term. every day we sailed forward, through choppy waves and thunderstorms, starvation and mutiny. we sailed ever forward. when we anchored, it was always temporary. this time, it was a beautiful island, dotted with palm trees, bordered by white sands. i didn't think i'd ever want to leave. i didn't think they'd leave without me.

ever since, i've laid alone on this beach. and though there was a sense of emptiness, of dread that tinged the salty air, it would feel almost romantic, the way the wind kissed the palm fronds and my feet kissed the sand and the waves kissed the shore and the sun kissed the waves.

but now the romance dissolved into despair and the sky is always washed with grey and the waves are always crashing and the fish always retreat when i approach and every time i step into the rising tide my feet sink deeper and deeper.

the ship isn't returning. i wonder if i'll be carried
away first by the wind, or the water. i wonder if
it's going to rain. i wonder when i started hating
the beach.

lonely.

i want to see with eyes unclouded
but the fog hangs so heavy over my head
thick with surviving wounds and guilt

the fear of love lost runs through my head
like blood racing through my veins
destroying all that i've worked for and built

and as i weave in and out of consciousness
i watch my loved ones drop off like flies
or flowers that have slowly begun to wilt

i am alone as always and always alone
a pain that fills so deeply in my heart
like a sword pushed up to the hilt

self-evaluation.

my singing voice is clear. a little high, but sweet.
i can't sing in front of people. sometimes the
weight of imperfection hangs so heavily on my
heart. i sing softly, i often get the words wrong.

my doodles are cute. they crop up in my
notebooks, on scrap pieces of paper. when i
draw, you can tell what it's supposed to be, but
it's never a masterpiece. i think my brain and
body have faulty connections, and i can never
fulfill the ideas i envision. i draw quickly, i erase
almost all of it.

my writing is bleak. dark and detailed, lacking in
metaphor and straight to the point. i think i get
so caught up in being understood that i forget to
be big and bold and unique. i don't know if i
could pick my own writing out of a line up. i
write often, i outgrow my words swiftly.

unclear.

clarity, while beautiful in its truth and simplicity, is far too raw and pure. blunt and sharp all at once, the lines are softer and less bloody that way. in any event, i smear the paint on the canvas, i pour water on the sidewalk chalk, i smudge the pencil marks on lined paper. i just want it to be blurry and dark. the discomfort of sitting with everything exactly as it is pierces deeper than any knife ever could. let me pretend it's anything else. let me twist it with my almost-correct metaphors, let me warp it with some slightly askew details. let me make this more palatable, let me make this pill easier to swallow.

dead or alive.

sometimes i think all i'll ever be is depressed.
because really, it's the only thing that stays
constant.
even in the happiness, the sadness is a spark of
paranoia and anxiety, nothing more than doubt
that i'll be able to maintain anything content or
fulfilling or passable as living.
and the spark grows into a flame grows into a
house fire crumbles into ash
and that ash is just the emptiness that remains
the carcass of joy that lived and breathed
the shell of a body that used to function
without being held up by the numbing and the
fog
in everything i do the depression is there
whether i'm feeling everything else, anything
else
but when i feel it, it's all i feel
its everything. often all i am is depressed.
so how can i be anything but?

panic.

day and night is the same to me
the sky hangs heavy endlessly
the stars and the sun are far too bright
and either way i hate the light

they bleed into each other like paints spilled on
my floor
i wait for them to stop spreading but they only
mix and stretch and my life is one long story,
one big mess on a once clean floor
no breaks or pauses or clean spots or chapter
breaks
i have no room to breathe, i am in an ocean of
notifications and grades and bank statements
and there is no end to the worries i have.
i am headed to a future darker than the night sky
my heart feels empty and desperately hopeless
and dreadful and nervous
11pm feels like 3am feels like 6pm feels like
1pm

worthless.

i exist only in the gaps in time where the
unimportant things happen
the small exchange between cashier and
customer, the awkward eye contact as you walk
past your neighbour walking their dog
i am only there in those moments, only noticed
by those who will never know me
i feel like once i am known, i am immediately
blocked out.
my words turn to static and my face becomes an
unrecognizable smudge
just a tiny blip in the smooth waves of a regular
life.
my existence is an imposition that is ignored and
unwanted by everyone.

happy belated to me.

i don't want to be another year older.

when i was 15 i was convinced i wouldn't live to be 20. i didn't even think i'd see 16.

tomorrow was a thought i couldn't even begin to fathom, a murky sea of sad sad sad that i didn't want to explore.

if there was a tomorrow, there was more pain. and my life was so permeated by grief and loss and confusion. another day was too much to bear.

but every day came like another beat in a song that refused to finish, a marching band that was dedicated to march right through to the end of the world, dragging me along like a corpse who couldn't object. but i was alive. i didn't dare object.

and things got better and worse and better and
worse and they got so good i thought i'd never
be pulled down, i'd float among the clouds like a
balloon that slipped from the clutches of a
toddler! and they got so bad i thought i couldn't
sink any lower, like an anchor dropped from the
highest possible point into the ocean,
plummeting through the deepest point and
burying myself in a lonely trench of sand and
hurt.

and i lived and i lived and i lived and i breathed
with lungs crumpled from emptiness and i spoke
with a throat sore from silence and i laughed and
i cried and i lived.

i couldn't stop myself from living.

my birthday is in 11 days, and i don't want to
turn 20.

not because of a fear of aging. although, living
til old age seems horribly embarrassing and
painful.

not because my teenage years were a movie that
i never wanted to end, most of it was spent
wallowing in loneliness.

not because of the impending unbearable load of adulthood and responsibility and independence and crippling loneliness.
okay. maybe a little because of that.

but my biggest issue with turning 20 is that i was never supposed to.

from the age of 15 i never bothered looking a day into my future because there could be nothing there. i didn't trust myself or the people around me or God to get myself to that point, to make it worthwhile or even possible.

i don't want to be 20 because i don't know how to.

still, i don't know how i'm supposed to live. and still, i don't really know if i want to.

change of heart.

how tiring it really is
to feel my life has reached its end
before it has even started,

my eyes shut with exhaustion
when the future feels pitch black
though truly, my effort is half-hearted.

but to decide to rebuff
this dreadful state, a state
from which i'll have soon departed,

i'll forge my own way
and cluelessly explore
these lands that are thus uncharted.

our hopes.

maybe we can hope that in the senselessness of
the sadness
there might be a seed of something better.

even through the wildfires that burn the trees in
the forest like matches in a box,
from the aged, gnarled oak to the frail, quivering
sapling
i hope there's a spray of buttery golden flowers
that survive the wretched heat
you hope for a shockingly green patch of grass
left standing among its wilted, burnt kin.

and through the ice age that freezes the water in
the earth like a hockey rink,
from the nearly dried up ponds to the oceans that
separate the continents
i hope there's a cleft for the salmon to gulp at air
you hope for a sunlit spot where the ice melts
faster than the rest.

and through the earthquakes that shuffle the
houses in town like decks of stiff playing cards
from the homely, ragged farm village to the
vain, crowded city.

i hope there's a library that keeps all the ancient
books in place on its shelves
you hope for a sturdy barn that protects its cattle
from the tremors.

nostalgia.

i miss the comfort of hopelessness
the weight of being nothing
freeing in that i knew there was nothing i could
do

i'm still tired like i've always been
but then there's the happiness
and there's more responsibility
something to maintain and a promise of more to
come

but the pressure of the melancholy
the threat of my wretched heart
darkening once more and losing its patience
is too much to bear at once

jigsaw.

i feel like for a while i became fragmented.
it's like the frame of my life shattered, and all the
pieces that made me who i am got all broken and
lost and warped.
i spent ages searching for every piece, working
on this ugly but familiar jigsaw every second of
every day.
but i grew without meaning to, an achingly slow
but constant process.
and eventually, the holes i couldn't fill, the
places where i couldn't make it fit right
everything ended up molding together again
once i became enough again to fill every piece

loveless.

growing without love stretches you out so thin that there are big yawning gaps in the places that are supposed to be complete and when the love floods in it makes everything feel too tight and crammed. how are you supposed to spread yourself out into a space you can barely fit into? you fold and contort yourself to be contained in those empty spaces that love couldn't fill before, there's no room for who you are without the love.

forgive me.

do you think my skin ever forgave the asphalt of
my elementary schoolyard? do you think my
eyes forgive the computer screen? do you think
my toes forgive the corner of the coffee table?
do you think my hair forgives the blades of my
barber's scissors?
because i'm slow to forgive. there was a time
when i'd blame myself for everything, using my
own body as a punching bag when i was
frustrated with the pain placed upon me. and
now i've turned that onto everyone else.
the problem is, my reaction when i'm hurt isn't
sadness, or concern. it's anger. and to forgive
from a place of anger is difficult. to know fully
how someone has hurt you, to know they
could've done differently. to let them get away
with it is hard.
but i suppose forgiveness is supposed to allow
you to let go of the pain yourself.
would forgiveness work if only i knew about it?
or does me not wanting them to know show i
haven't really forgiven them at all?
how am i supposed to let my anger fade without
letting people walk all over me?

how am i supposed to let my anger fade towards
myself? how can i forgive someone who will
never let me?

welcome home.

i think i am easy to know.
my heart is unlocked, and an oak sign shouts the
words "COME ON IN!" in big block letters,
planted in the grass by the front door.
there's not a bare wall to be seen, they're all
plastered with outdated photographs and dried
flowers and poetry passages and mediocre
artwork.
there's no hardwood or tiling, but a deep blue
carpeting i pretend is the ocean, and a striped
furniture set like the pajamas those bananas
wore.
there's nothing at the bottom of the stairs to the
basement besides an eggshell grandfather clock
with a body that opens up, revealing small
shelves with dead batteries and heavy dust.
and in the living room, there's a baby grand
piano that creaks from disuse, keys out of tune,
pages of sheet music crumpled beneath the piano
bench for songs i'll never play again.
my heart is unlocked, and a small embroidery
hoop hangs on the inside of the door, whispering
"please come again soon..." in tiny,
hand-stitched cursive.
i think i am easy to know.
i fear no one will ever want to.

shipwrecked redux.

how long ago was the storm?
the swarm of coarse winds that slashed through
our ship
the wall of desperate words and bodies packed
dense like sardines on deck
the icy shock of the water careening into our life
boat as we were hurled into the waves.

we held hands the first few hours to keep each
other in the raft
our other palms flush with the gummy rubber
tubing on the inside.
when we finally untangle our fingers
my palm screams red with the crescents of your
nails.

we sunbathe every day with our eyes pressed
shut
telling each other stories of where we were in
another universe
and pretending it could be real
when i open my eyes to look over at you
your eyes are closed, but you're smiling.

good morning.

today i woke up rather early,
and my blankets had stayed in their place,
i told myself that it'd be a good day
then i got up to go wash my face.

i fried bacon and eggs on the stovetop,
filled the kettle with water for tea
i heard rain as i ate up my breakfast,
and watched Arthur on my tv

mornings were hopeless and tired,
so i'd sleep til the day was near done,
but lately i've taken to waking up early,
and watching the rise of the sun.

www.ingramcontent.com/pod-product-compliance
Lightning Source LLC
Chambersburg PA
CBHW050750180726
48003CB00020B/2323